REMINISCENCES—1861 to 1865

An Adventure With Guerrillas.

GIVING A TRUE ACCOUNT OF THE CAPTURE AND
KILLING OF A PARTY OF UNION TROOPS
BY THE GUERRILLAS.

By ETHELBIRT CROUSE,

OF THE 130th INDIANA VOLUNTEERS.

THIRD EDITION.

Published by Grand Teuton Press
844 Loraine
Grosse Pointe, MI 48230

ISBN: 978-0-557-49315-9

Introduction to the Third Edition -

This is a very slightly edited version of the second edition of An Adventure With Guerrillas - a few misspellings have been corrected, but no changes have been made to the original sense or choice of words. A complete facsimile of the 1899 edition (the second edition) follows the current one.

I remember reading this little book as a boy, and even remembered some of the scenes when rereading it as I transcribed it for this volume, but the effect it had on me now is immeasurably stronger than it had been then.

No doubt a good part of that difference lies in the fact that my son is currently serving in the U.S. Army, making any such story just that much more immediate. However, I think much of the power came from the author's straightforward and matter-of-fact relation of events which he plainly attributed to the direct intervention of God.

It was largely that unabashed, unashamed acknowledgment of God's Providence that set this story apart from the other war reminiscences I've read, and which made it all the more important to me that it get back into print.

The author, Ethelbirt Crouse, is my great-great-grandfather on my mother's mother's mother's side of the family, and a faded photocopy of the 1899 edition is all that we had left. I hope, dear reader, that you will find this story as moving as I do, and that you will pass it on to generations to come.

Charles J. van Becelaere
June 2010
Grosse Pointe, Michigan

Ethelbirt Crouse

AN ADVENTURE WITH GUERRILLAS.

As I have been repeatedly asked to give an account of my experience as a soldier, and more especially my adventure with Bushwhackers while in the service during the late war, I have concluded to do so, in my own way, as I make no pretense to being a literary man, but will tell a "plain, unvarnished tale," and respectfully ask that all imperfections may be overlooked.

I ENLISTED on the 6th of November, 1863. at Ossian, Wells county, Indiana, at the age of sixteen, under James A. Milliken, who was authorized by Governor Morton, of Indiana, to enlist recruits for the volunteer service. He was afterward elected captain. On the 19th of November we went to Kokomo, Indiana, where we were organized as a company (F) in the 130th Regiment Indiana Volunteer Infantry. We were sworn in on the 29th day of December. March 1st, 1864, we started for the field in Tennessee, via Indianapolis, and Louisville, Kentucky; arrived at Nashville in due time; then made a twenty days' march into East Tennessee, and joined the 23d Army Corps at Charleston. Our regiment was in Hovey's Division, and nick-named "Hovey's Babies." Went through the Atlanta campaign, and when Hood came back to Nashville we followed back.

Our corps was divided – one part went to Columbia and Franklin, Tennessee; the part I belonged to was sent to Johnsonville to reinforce some colored troops on the Tennessee river. There we lay for some time, and as usual, built winter quarters.

On the 20th day of November five regiments in command of General Cooper of Tennessee, started on a forced march for Columbia, Tennessee, and by permission of my captain, while in line of march, I fell out of rank to get a drink of water; my blanket and the rest of my accoutrements were very wet, as it was raining all the time. I did not catch up with the command that day; that night I fell in with five of my company, Isaac Caston, Louis Hendry, Joseph King, Adam Humbaugh and Lemuel N. Grandstaff, and we all slept together in a corn house that night. We were out of rations, having eaten the last the day before, and could not forage any, for we had been informed that there were guerrillas in that locality, and we found it to be so, all too soon. We looked for turnip patches along the road, but did not enter a house, and I found that when a man was on a march of that kind, he wanted more than turnips for a day and a half. On Sunday, the 27th, about nine or ten o'clock, we found that the guerrillas were in pursuit of us, so we started to run, and ran until about eleven o'clock. When we were within a quarter mile of our rear guards they attacked us. Our guns were loaded but would not go off, our ammunition being wet; we tried to fire at them as they came up, but was of no use; when we started to run some could not run as fast as others. There were four of us, but they captured thirteen in all.

When we found our guns would not go off, King threw away his knapsack and gun and left us. I tried the same, but did not succeed; the first I knew I was surrounded by nine or ten of the villains. They wore no uniforms and were dressed in citizens' clothes, and were armed with shotguns, rifles, carbines, muskets and revolvers. They asked me for my gun. I told them it was in the rear, as I had thrown it away with my knapsack when I attempted to run. They ordered me to get it, and went back with me to find it, and when I picked it up the saw it was bent and asked what did it. I told them I did. They asked why I bent the gun? I answered, because it would not go off. They ordered me to throw it away as it would be of no use to them. They next asked me for my pocketbook. I gave it to them. They said give us your pistol and knife. I told them I had none. They told me not to be scared for they intended to parole me and send me home. Some of them followed King but did not get him. He had got into a deep ravine and ran into a field where there was a planter and some colored men at work. The planter drew his pistol and ordered him to halt, he asked King where he was going to and where he belonged, and King told him, supposing him to be friendly; but the planter shot him down. The colored men wanted to bury him but the planter told them if they touched the Yankee son-of-a-b---, he would shoot them. I never learned what became of the poor fellow's remains.

When they found they could not catch King they returned to the party who had taken me back to where Caston, Hendry and Grandstaff were. Humbaugh was still further back, as will be noted. They then marched us back about eleven miles, where they had some more of our boys; they were on horses, and made us "double quick" all the way. They took us through the fields and over the fences, purposely avoiding the roads – fearing Union cavalry, no doubt. We had to take down and put up the fences. They kept telling us not to be scared, they would do us no harm, for they would parole us and send us home; and so they did, but such a paroling I never want to see again!

After they got us where they "paroled us," as they called it, they had in all thirteen of us, surrounded so thick we could not get out without running over some of them, they were joined by some more of the villains who came up with a first lieutenant that some of our boys had wounded in the side, and who afterwards died. About this time two old men came riding up to us and said, with a cackle, "You have got some of the Yankee sons-of-b----s, we see, and we suppose you know what to do with them?" They said they did.

In a few minutes they drew us up in a line, and made us tell off in whole numbers from right to left, and then divided us into squads, making two squads containing four men each, and one squad containing five men. The last squad, of five men (all strangers to me as to their names, excepting one man, a sergeant belonging to the 25th Michigan Regiment whose name I cannot now call to mind), were marched off into a hollow and shot, one by one, no time being given them for preparation to make their peace with God: no chance to write a last word of farewell to relatives or friends in God's country. The fiends in human guise made use of a navy revolver as the instrument of death. When we heard the shots, Caston said he felt uneasy, when the man the rebs called sergeant said, "Well you might if you knew what I do." Says Grandstaff, "You took those men out to shoot them." He replied, with a cackle, "We did, and we intend to serve you the same way." Readers, imagine if you can how we felt then! Says Caston, "I wish to make one request, and that is for you to wrap us three (meaning himself, Hendry his cousin, and myself) in one blanket and bury us together, as we were raised together." And they said they would, but they did not.

The second squad of four was Hendry, Grandstaff, a soldier whose name was unknown to me, and myself. Just as they started with us the unknown soldier began to run. He was fired upon, and seven balls struck him before he fell, so that gave us warning not to attempt to run. We offered to do anything for them; we prayed and begged of them to spare our lives, but all in vain; we might as well have prayed to blocks of wood or stone.

They laughed at us and mocked us in our woe and misery, and told us we ought to have thought of the probability of getting into just such trouble before we left our homes. They then marched us off a few rods in an opposite direction from that to which the first squad were taken. We stood by a tree until the villain loaded the revolver. One man did all the shooting; he was a young man about seventeen years old, and he did his work as cheerfully as a man would in shooting a lot of hogs. When he was ready he ordered us to turn our backs; three of us obeyed his order, but Caston said he had humbled himself to them all he was going to, so one of the villains behind shot him, and then the young villain shot Hendry, and then came my turn. I had often wondered, when reading of military executions, of hangings, of death by the guillotine and various other methods of executing men, how such men felt when they knew that only an instant's time was theirs before they would be hurried into eternity – into that unknown land whence no traveler returns. How I felt is almost beyond my power of telling, but suffice it to say, that it came very forcibly to me that I had done my utmost duty for my country as a soldier, but above all was the memory of HOME and MOTHER; and I would have prayed, but no time was given for that, I immediately repeated a verse from an old familiar song, which all soldiers know: the chorus being:

> "Farewell mother, you may never press me to your heart again,
> But you'll not forget me, mother, if I'm numbered with the slain."

And yet there was a feeling – a faint hope that I might escape through some defect in the shooting party. I posed myself for the fatal shot by leaning slightly forward, crossing my hands upon my breast, and closing my eyes. The pistol was snapped five times before it went off, the ball striking me through the left ear, close to my head, grazing the cord and rendering me numb and senseless.

Grandstaff, who was on my left and ahead of me, said I received the shot without flinching. I fell forward on my face. He then shot Grandstaff, the ball striking him above the left ear, not entering the skull, and lodged above the left eye. He fell forward on his face, but not senseless. They then brought the third squad and shot them the same as they had us, one by one. I did not know but one of that squad, and he was Humbaugh, a mere boy, only fourteen and a half years old. Grandstaff said he begged most pitifully until the pistol cracked and he fell dead. Then when they had completed their devilish work, and we were all dead, as they supposed, they commenced rifling our pockets. One of them came to me and turned me on my back, which restored me to consciousness; he cut the buttons off my coat, then ran his hand into my side pocket for some things I had not given up, and I think he discovered that I was alive by my heart-beat, for he said with an oath, "This son of a b~~h is not dead, I will show him how to play off on me!" He was standing astride of me. He stepped one step back; his right foot was against my left foot; he then drew his pistol and cocked it. When I heard the click I opened my eyes and looked into the muzzle, and when it went off I shut my eyes, stretched my hands out, and quivered my fingers. He said with an oath, "Now he is dead! See him clinch his hands!" Another said: "His brains flew in my face." I knew that was not so, but refrained from telling them, for very prudent reasons. I was rational all the time, after he turned me over, and the last shot entered my throat on the left side of my windpipe and lodged

7

under the left jaw, and there it still remains, and will no doubt remain until my dying day, a constant reminder of our "erring brethren," whom we are asked to forgive and forget!

We lay there about thirty minutes. I raised my head and Grandstaff said, "Lay still, they are not far away." He then asked, "Are you hurt much?" I said I was shot twice but can get away. I asked him if he was hurt bad? He said he was. I tried to get up but could not. I made the third attempt before I could stand. Then I started up the hill, holding to trees as I went, and my comrade followed. We did not know where we were, but I took the lead and was guided by an unseen power. It seemed as though I must go that way. My vision may have been injured by the wounds I had received, but, nevertheless, a very strange thing happened to me. There was continually before me a steady, white radiance, not as light as sunlight, but brighter than moonlight. The night was very dark. Soldiers who have been in southern forests of pine, know how intensely dark it is when there is no moon or stars. It was sleeting, and we trudged on through the pitiless storm, but the light guided us and kept us from running against trees. The first thought that struck me was to keep off the road and trail they brought us in on. The road and trail were about four miles apart. When we had gone about one mile my comrade thought he could go no farther. He said, "I have but one death to die," and he laid down. "I cannot go any farther," he said. I told him he could, and taking

8

hold of him dragged him through the mud and water for six or eight feet. He said, "help me up and let me take hold of your arm, and I will go along with you." I felt as if I could not bear to leave any more comrades behind than I had. He was not shot as bad as I was, but the excitement kept me up. After I got warmed up I felt as though the best horse the rebs had could not catch me on a fair foot race. We kept in all the water we could to throw any bloodhounds off our track should they send any out, as they might be human enough to return to bury us, and finding Grandstaff and myself missing, would send hounds on our trail. We made fifteen miles that night, when we came to Pine River. We traveled along the bank some distance until we came to a point where we thought we could cross. I told my comrade to stand on the bank until I waded out in it and made the crossing all right. Now right here I cannot refrain from mentioning something that has, and will ever seem very strange to me. I cannot swim a stroke, never having learned, being from boyhood afraid of water; but in this instance I waded boldly in, and Pine River being a very swift stream, before I got across I had to bend my head back to keep the water from running into my mouth. I would not like to undertake the same again, unless it was to save my life. I told my comrade to wait until I got across and I would make a noise and then he could follow. I did so, and he attempted to cross, but the current carried him downstream. I held to a bush and waded in until the water came to my mouth as it had done before, and got hold of him and helped him out.

We found we had a very steep hill to climb. My comrade said, "We can never get up," but knowing I must contradict him, said, "Yes, we can. You go ahead and I will follow you and push you with my head." And so we went up the hill on "all fours," which took us about an hour. When we arrived at the top we rested for a few moments, the white light, which I have before mentioned, still continued, and I aimed to strike the road near where we were captured, and I think we did not miss it more than ten rods.

Now, I think for a boy, or two boys, rather, to travel eleven miles through the woods - the odd four miles being along roads - for that distance, there must have been something more than human power to have guided us. Talk about praying - we had not been praying boys previous to this - but if any one ever felt the need of prayer we did then, and we did the best we could. When we wanted a drink we just "stooped" down in the road and took it, and that was pretty often, as we were bleeding most of the time. After we struck the road we frequently thought we had come to cross roads. I would get down and hunt for a wagon track, or a horse or mule track, and when I found it, I said in a low tone to my pard, "This is the way." Some may say, where was the mysterious light you have heretofore spoken of? It only remained with us while we were in the woods.

We were now evidently approaching a picket line, for my comrade said: "Birt, I see a light in the mountains." I answered "it was nothing but foxfire, and now I want you to come on, if we are attacked we will keep together and perhaps we will not be captured." He said, "Listen, I hear something." I said, "No, you don't, now come on;" and I think we had not gone ahead more than fifteen feet until three musket shots were fired on us. The first shot the powder burned my face, and the flash of the guns shown upon us so that one of the men thought he could catch us, and he made the attempt and dropped his gun, but we got out of his way. There was no time for us to consult where to run. I went over a fence, just how I cannot tell, but over I went, and down a hill or bank into a field and threw myself into some weeds, or rather "kuckel burs;" they stuck me all over, but that was nothing. I laid there and prayed more earnestly than ever.

I said, "My God! my God! after I have gone through with what I have, must I die here?" when I seemed to hear a voice say, "Trust in Me, I will bear you through!" and I laid as easily as I could under the circumstances. In a few minutes I dropped asleep from utter weariness and exhaustion, and dreamed that those men who had fired on us were Union troops, and in a few minutes, so it seemed to me (it must have been fully two hours), I was aroused by the bugle playing the reveille. It was so near through playing when I was fully awake, I could not determine the direction of the sound, but I felt I was safe! In a few moments the same good old bugle played the call to "tear down tent!" It sounded sweeter to me than any dinner horn I ever heard; I knew the sound of it then, it belonged to the brigade we were in. It was not yet quite daylight, so I laid still until the third call was sounded, and then I thought I must obey and fall in; I made three attempts before I could stand on my feet, and then started out. I went very carefully now, for I knew the pickets had not been taken off, as it was not light enough to see a man to distinguish friend from foe, any distance. The picket halted me before I got to the fence, and said: "Who comes there?" I said, "Friend, without the countersign." The next question was, "How did you come there?" and I answered, saying: "I was captured yesterday, and have been shot twice by guerrillas." "Where do you belong?" said the picket, and I answered: "Co. F. 130th Regiment Indiana Volunteers, Colonel C. S. Parrish, Third Brigade, Third Division, Twenty-third Army Corps." Said the picket: "We belong to that; advance, friend, with your hands up." And I did so, but I could not get over the fence. They asked if it was me the other relief had fired upon. I told them it was. They said the reason they had done so was because they had been attacked last night by guerrillas, and their orders were to fire on anything without halting it. I told them I had a partner out there some place. "I wish you would find him and tell him I am safe, and tell him to come on. Tell me how far it is to my regiment." "It is about one mile," said they; "you had better stop at General Cooper's headquarters and report." I did so. The first men I saw that I knew were Lieutenant W. H. Covert and Curtis Burgin from my company. They did not know me, and the first words they said were: "My God! pardner! what is the matter?" I told them in as

12

short a way as I could, as it was very difficult and painful for me to talk. The General ordered one of them to put me on a horse and take me to my regiment. I told them I could walk better than I could ride, as the motion of the horse would give me much pain.

They were going to move the command, and were dividing it there; part of it going up Duck River under command of Gen. Cooper, and part, under Col. Parrish was to remain there, consisting of two regiments – our own regiment and the 99th Ohio, and half of the artillery. I found my regiment on a large hill. When I arrived at the foot of the hill I could not go any further, so I laid down by the side of a path and said to myself, "That is the hardest mile I ever traveled." I had not lain there but a short time when one of my company boys, Ambrose Hammans, second duty sergeant, came down the hill after water, and he repeated the lieutenant's words, saying, "My God! pard, what is the matter? Where do you belong?" Said I, "I am Birt Crouse; I want you to help me up the hill; I can't talk much." He said, "I will go and call some of the boys; you are not fit to walk." He went to the top of the hill and fairly yelled: "Company F, Birt is down here and is all shot to pieces, and the worse sight you ever saw to be living, and he wants to get up the hill." I never will forget the way he sang this out, in his excited manner, and not only the company, but all that were within the sound of his voice came: some did not wait to dress, but as they had slept, some dressing as they ran, and better looking faces I thought I never had seen.

They sympathized with me as much as brothers.

The regimental surgeon dressed my wounds and said to my captain, "Are you acquainted with his folks?" The captain said he was. Said the surgeon, "find out if he wants to send word home, for he will never live to see 10 o'clock." The captain was a noble man, always ready to help any of his men out of trouble. He came and sat by me in the little dog tent and said, "Birt, I want to talk to you a little." I told my story as briefly as I could, and that I wanted him to send some men to find Grandstaff, "send a pretty good squad and arm them," I said, "and bring them to me before they go out, for I want to give them orders." He said, "Ambrose, detail thirty men and a sergeant, and see that their guns are all in good order." But he did not have to make the detail, he had more volunteers than he knew what to do with. They were furnished with forty rounds of ammunition to each man, and were brought to me for orders, and I said: "Boys, you are going in a particular place, you have never fought those villains, and so I say to you boys, if you are attacked, fight for life, you can see how they have served me." And so they went.

"Birt," said the captain, "do you want to send any word home? If so, what is it? You can't live long." I said, "No, I am all right, if I can only get some rest. So please don't bother me." Our parents had lived near each other for many years, and when I enlisted he had promised my father that he would watch over me, and hence his anxiety to do something for me, and I had to send him away so often that at last I got so tired that I sent for the colonel, who was away when I was brought in, and knew nothing of my condition. And when he came to see me and learned what I wanted, he cried like a child, and asked what he could do for me. I told him I could not tell him how I felt, but, said I, "Colonel, I want rest; can you fix it so I can get it?" He said, "Yes," and turning to the captain, said: "We must put a guard over our boy, he begs so for rest, and I feel I must do all I can for him, for God knows he has seen enough." The guards were brought, and their orders were to allow no one but the man who waited upon me to come near me. So then I rested as well as could be expected, and I laid there until about 4 o'clock, but felt too bad to eat. They talked to me for a while, and I went to sleep and rested pretty well that night. In the morning, which was Tuesday, the 29th, my nurse, Robert G. Rogers, now living at Ossian, Ind., a noble fellow, got some corn meal and made a gruel, which he fed me with a spoon, and you may believe it tasted good, as I had eaten nothing since we were captured, which took place about 11 o'clock, Sunday, the 27th, as before stated.

We were at that time cut off from all communication, so we remained there for a few days and then started on a forced march for Franklin, Tenn. The squad of men who were sent out to hunt Grandstaff had been gone three days and had not found him, but on the fourth day we received a dispatch stating that he was up the river with the general's command, had the ball taken out, and was doing well. We had just so many hours in which to reach Franklin in order to get ahead of Hood, but did not make it, and so the battle of Franklin, or Columbia, as some called it, was fought.

We only got in sight of the town and captured one picket post; they did not fire a gun. We came to a halt and found the rebels lay around us in the shape of a horseshoe. It was about 10 o'clock at night when we captured the post and they were just starting their camp fires and supposed we were some of their own army moving. Our officers held a council how to get out; they were gathered around the wagon I was in, and I heard them say, "We can make a dash and get our men through, but we cannot get our artillery and wagons through;" and then they went away, and I went out of the back of that wagon, saying, "If this wagon is not going, I don't belong to it; where is my regiment?" "You have been there enough, haven't you," says the Colonel, "but we are not going to go through. You stay in the wagon, and if we conclude to make the attempt I will come and let you know." But I was afraid they might forget me, so he directed me to my regiment, and directions were given us how to make a retrograde movement, and we did so. We got out of the horseshoe without any noise, no gun was fired, and not a mule brayed. We crossed the Cumberland River near Clarksville, Tenn., at which place I was put upon a hospital boat (we marched 84 miles after leaving the vicinity of Franklin), and I remained on the boat until I was able to do duty, which was about six months, and then I joined my regiment at Charlotte, N. C., in June, 1865. At the close of the war a partial account of our affair with the Bushwhackers was published in the Louisville Journal, the same being furnished by our boat surgeon.

Here follows a facsimile of the full second edition as I have it.

Unfortunately, it is from a fairly poor-quality photocopy (probably a second or third generation copy at that).

Still, it is basically legible, and gives us an interesting view of turn-of-the-last-century publishing practices, and would that we could still publish it for ten cents!

REMINISCENCES--1861 to 1865

An Adventure With Guerrillas.

GIVING A TRUE ACCOUNT OF THE CAPTURE AND
KILLING OF A PARTY OF UNION TROOPS
BY THE GUERRILLAS.

By ETHELBIRT CROUSE,

OF THE 130th INDIANA VOLUNTEERS.

SECOND EDITION.

Price, - - 10 Cents.

ANTWERP, OHIO:
Published by A. N. Smith, Argus Office,
1899.

AN ADVENTURE WITH GUERRILLAS.

As I have been repeatedly asked to give an account of my experience as a soldier, and more especially my adventure with Bushwhackers while in the service during the late war, I have concluded to do so, in my own way, as I make no pretense to being a literary man, but will tell a "plain, unvarnished tale," and respectfully ask that all imperfections may be overlooked.

I ENLISTED on the 6th of November, 1863. at Ossian, Wells county. Indiana, at the age of sixteen, under James A. Milliken, who was authorized by Governor Morton, of Indiana, to enlist recruits for the volunteer service. He was afterward elected captain. On the 19th of November we went to Kokomo, Indiana, where we were organized as a company (F) in the 130th Regiment Indiana Volunteer Infantry. We were sworn in on the 29th day of December. March 1st, 1864, we started for the field in Tennessee, via Indianapolis, and Louisville, Kentucky; arrived at Nashville in due time; then made a twenty days' march into East Tennessee, and joined the 23d Army Corps at Charleston. Our regiment was in Hovey's Division, and nic-named "Hovey's Babies." Went through the Atlanta campaign, and when Hood came back to Nashville we followed back.

Our corps was divided—one part went to Columbia and Franklin, Tennessee; the part I belonged to was sent to Johnsonville to reinforce some colored troops on the Tennessee river. There we lay for some time, and as usual, built winter quarters.

On the 20th day of November five regiments in command of General Cooper of Tennessee, started on a forced march for Columbia, Tennessee, and by permission of my captain, while in line of march, I fell out of rank to get a drink of water; my blanket and the rest of my accoutrements were very wet, as it was raining all the time. I did not catch up with the command that day; that night I fell in with five of my company, Isaac Caston, Louis Hendry, Joseph King, Adam Humbaugh and Lemuel N. Grandstaff, and we all slept together in a corn house that night. We were out of rations, having eaten the last the day before, and could not forage any, for we had been informed that there were guerillas in that locality, and we found it to be so, all too soon. We looked for turnip patches along the road, but did not enter a house, and I found that when a man was on a march of that kind, he wanted more than turnips for a day and a half. On Sunday, the 27th, about nine or ten o'clock, we found that the guerrillas were in pursuit of us, so we started to run, and ran until about eleven o'clock. When we were within a quarter of a mile of our rear guards they attacked us. Our guns were loaded but would not go off, our ammunition being wet; we tried to fire at them as they came up, but was of no use; when we started to run some could not run as fast as others. There were four of us, but they captured thirteen in all. When we found our guns would not go off, King threw away his knapsack and gun and left us. I tried the same, but did not succeed; the first I knew I was surrounded by nine or ten of the villains. They wore no uniforms and were dressed in citizens clothes, and were armed with shot guns, rifles, carbines, muskets and revolvers. They asked me for my gun. I told them it was in the rear, as I had thrown it away with my knapsack when I attempted to run. They ordered me to get it, and went back with me to find it, and when I picked it up they saw it was bent and asked what did it. I told them I did. They asked why I bent the gun? I answered, because it would not go off. They ordered me to throw it away as it would be of no use to them. They next asked me for my pocketbook. I gave it to them. They said give us your pistol and knife. I told them I had none. They told me not to be scared for they intended to parole me and send me home. Some of them followed King but did not get him. He had got into a deep ravine and ran into a field where there was a planter and some colored men at work. The planter drew his pistol and ordered him to halt, he asked King where he was going to and where he belonged, and King told him, supposing him to be friendly; but the planter shot him down. The colored men wanted to bury him but the planter told them if they touched the yankee son-of-a-b—, he would shoot them. I never learned what became of the poor fellow's remains.

When they found they could not catch King they returned to the party who had taken me back to where Caston, Hendry and Grendstaff were. Humbaugh was still further back, as will be noted. They then marched us back about eleven miles, where they had some more of our boys; they were on horses, and made us "double quick" all the way. They took us through the fields and over the fences, purposely avoiding the roads—fearing Union cavalry, no doubt. We had to take down and put up the fences They kept telling us not to be scared, they would do us no harm, for they would parole us and send us home; and so they did, but such a paroling I never want to see again!

After they got us where they "paroled us," as they called it, they had in all thirteen of us, surrounded so thick we could not get out without running over some of them, they were joined by some more of the villians who came up with a first lieutenant that some of our boys had wounded in the side, and who afterwards died. About this time two old men came riding up to us and said, with a cackle, "You have got some of the Yankee sons-of-b—s, we see, and we suppose you know what to do with them?" They said they did.

In a few minutes they drew us up in a line, and made us tell off in whole numbers from right to left, and then divided us into squads, making two squads containing four men each, and one squad containing five men. The last squad, of five men (all strangers to me as to their names, excepting one man, a sergeant belonging to the 25th Michigan Regiment, whose name I can not now call to mind), were marched off into a hollow and shot, one by one, no time being given them for preparation to make their peace with God: no chance to write a last word of farewell to relatives or friends in God's country. The fiends in human guise made use of a navy revolver as the instrument of death When we heard the shots, Caston said he felt uneasy, when the man the rebs called sergeant said, "Well you might if you knew what I do." Says Grandsaff, "You took those men out to shoot them." He replied, with a cackle. "We did, and we intend to serve you the same way." Readers, imagine if you can how we felt then! Says Caston, "I wish to make one request, and that is for you to wrap us three (meaning himself, Hendry his cousin, and myself) in one blanket and bury us together, as we were raised together." And they said they would, but they did not.

The second squad of four was Hendry, Grandstaff, a soldier whose name was unknown to me, and myself. Just as they started with us the unknown soldier began to run. He was fired upon, and seven balls struck him before he fell, so that gave us warning not to attempt to run. We offered to do anything for them; we prayed and begged of them to spare our lives, but all in vain; we might as well have prayed to blocks of wood or stone.

They laughed at us and mocked us in our woe and misery, and told us we ought to have thought of the probability of getting into just such trouble before we left our homes. They then marched us off a few rods in an opposite direction from that to which the first squad were taken. We stood by a tree until the villian loaded the revolver. One man did all the shooting; he was a young man about seventeen years old, and he did his work as cheerfully as a man would in shooting a lot of hogs. When he was ready he ordered us to turn our backs; three of us obeyed his order, but Caston said he had humbled himself to them all he was going to, so one of the villians behind shot him, and then the young villian shot Hendry, and then came my turn. I had often wondered, when reading of military executions, of hangings, of death by the guillotine and various other methods of executing men, how such men felt when they knew that only an instant's time was theirs before they would be hurried into eternity—into that unknown land whence no traveler returns. How I felt is almost beyond my power of telling, but suffice it to say, that it came very forcibly to me that I had done my utmost duty for my country as a soldier, but above all was the memory of HOME and MOTHER; and I would have prayed, but no time was given for that, I immediatly repeated a verse from an old familiar song, which all soldiers know; the chorus being:

"Farewell mother, you may never press me to your heart again,

But you'll not forget me, mother, if I'm numbered with the
  slain."

And yet there was a feeling—a faint hope that I
might escape through some defect in the shooting
party. I posed myself for the fatal shot by leaning
slightly forward, crossing my hands upon my breast
and closing my eyes. The pistol was snapped five
times before it went off, the ball striking me through
the left ear, close to my head, grazing the cord and
rendering me numb and senseless. Grandstaff, who
was on my left and ahead of me, said I received the
shot without flinching. I fell forward on my face.
He then shot Grandstaff, the ball striking him above
the left ear, not entering the skull, and lodged above
the left eye. He fell forward on his face, but not
senseless. They then brought the third squad and
shot them the same as they had us, one by one. I
did not know but one of that squad, and he was
Humbaugh, a mere boy, only fourteen and a half
years old. Grandstaff said he begged most pitifully
until the pistol cracked and he fell dead. Then when
they had completed their develish work, and we were
all dead, as they supposed, they commenced rifling
our pockets. One of them came to me and turned
me on my back, which restored me to consciousness;
he cut the buttons off my coat, then ran his hand into my side pocket for some things I had not given
up, and I think he discovered that I was alive by my
heart-beat, for he said with an oath, "This son of a
b—h is not dead, I will show him how to play off on
me!" He was standing astride of me. He stepped
one step back; his right foot was against my left foot;
he then drew his pistol and cocked it. When I heard
the click I opened my eyes and looked into the muzzle, and when it went off I shut my eyes, stretched
my hands out and quivered my fingers. He said with
an oath, "Now he is dead! See him clinch his
hands!" Another said: "His brains flew in my face."

I knew that was not so, but refrained from telling them, for very prudent reasons. I was rational all the time, after he turned me over, and the last shot entered my throat on the left side of my windpipe and lodged under the left jaw, and there it still remains, and will no doubt remain until my dying day, a constant reminder of our "erring brethren," whom we are asked to forgive and forget!

We lay there about thirty minutes. I raised my head and Grandstaff said, "Lay still, they are not far away." He then asked, "Are you hurt much?" I said I was shot twice, but I can get away. I asked him if he was hurt bad? He said he was. I tried to get up but could not. I made the third attempt before I could stand. Then I started up the hill, holding to trees as I went, and my comrade followed. We did not know where we were, but I took the lead and was guided by an unseen power. It seemed as though I must go that way. My vision may have been injured by the wounds I had received, but, nevertheless, a very strange thing happened to me. There was continually before me a steady, white radiance, not as light as sunlight, but brighter than moonlight. The night was very dark. Soldiers who have been in southern forests of pine, know how intensely dark it is when there is no moon or stars. It was sleeting, and we trudged on through the pitiless storm, but the light guided us and kept us from running against trees. The first thought that struck me was to keep off the road and trail they brought us in on. The road and trail were about four miles apart. When we had gone about one mile my comrade thought he could go no farther. He said, "I have but one death to die," and he laid down. "I cannot go any further," he said. I told him he could, and taking hold of him dragged him through the mud and water for six or eight feet. He said, "help me up and let me take hold of your arm, and I will go along with you." I felt as if I could not bear to leave any more comrades behind than I had. He was not shot as bad as I was, but the excitement kept me up. After I got warmed up I felt as though the best horse the rebs had could not catch me on a fair foot race. We kept in all the water we could to throw any bloodhounds off our track should they send any out, as they might be human enough to return to bury us, and finding Grandstaff and myself missing, would send hounds on our trail. We made fifteen miles that night, when we came to Pine River. We traveled along the bank some distance until we came to a point where we thought we could cross. I told my comrade to stand on the bank until I waded out in it and made the crossing all right. Now right here I cannot refrain from mentioning something that has, and will ever seem very strange to me. I cannot swim a stroke, never having learned, being from boyhood afraid of water; but in this instance I waded boldly in, and Pine River being a very swift stream, before I got across I had to bend my head back to keep the water from running into my mouth. I would not like to undertake the same again, unless it was to save my life. I told my comrade to wait until I got across and I would make a noise and then he could follow. I did so, and he attempted to cross, but the current carried him down stream. I held to a bush and waded in until the water came up to my mouth as it had done before, and got hold of him and helped him out. We found we had a very steep hill to climb. My comrade said, "We can never get up," but knowing I must contradict him, said, "Yes, we can. You go ahead and I will follow you and push you with my head." And so we went up the hill on "all fours," which took us about an hour. When we arrived at the top we rested for a few moments, the white light, which I have before mentioned, still continued, and I aimed to strike the road near where we were captured, and I think we did not miss it more than ten rods.

Now, I think for a boy, or two boys, rather, to travel eleven miles through the woods—the odd four miles being along roads—for that distance, there must have been something more than human power to have guided us. Talk about praying—we had not been praying boys previous to this—but if any one ever felt the need of prayer we did then, and we did the best we could. When we wanted a drink we just "stooped" down in the road and took it, and that was pretty often, as we were bleeding most of the time. After we struck the road we frequently thought we had come to cross roads. I would get down and hunt for a wagon track, or a horse or mule track, and when I found it, I said in a low tone to my pard, "This is the way." Some may say, where was the mysterious light you have heretofore spoken of? It only remained with us while we were in the woods.

We were now evidently approaching a picket line, for my comrade said: "Birt, I see a light in the mountains." I answered "it was nothing but fox-fire, and now I want you to come on, if we are attacked we will keep together and perhaps we will not be captured." He said, "Listen, I hear something." I said, "No, you don't. now come on;" and I think we had not gone ahead more than fifteen feet until three musket shots were fired on us. The first shot the powder burned my face, and the flash of the guns shown upon us so that one of the men thought he could catch us. and he made the attempt and dropped his gun, but we got out of his way. There was no time for us to consult where to run. I went over a fence, just how I cannot tell, but over I went, and down a hill or bank into a field and threw myself into some weeds, or rather "kuckel burs;" they stuck me all over, but that was nothing. I laid there and prayed more earnestly than ever.

I said, "My God! my God! after I have gone through with what I have, must I die here?" when I seemed to hear a voice say, "Trust in Me, I will bear you through!" and I laid as easily as I could under the circumstances. In a few minutes I dropped asleep from utter weariness and exhaustion, and dreamed that those men who had fired on us were Union troops, and in a few minutes, so it seemed to me (it must have been fully two hours), I was aroused by the bugle playing the reveille. It was so near through playing when I was fully awake, I could not determine the direction of the sound, but I felt I was safe! In a few moments the same good old bugle played the call to "tear down tent!" It sounded sweeter to me than any dinner horn I ever heard; I knew the sound of it then, it belonged to the brigade we were in. It was not yet quite daylight, so I laid still until the third call was sounded, and then I thought I must obey and fall in; I made three attempts before I could stand on my feet, and then started out. I went very carefully now, for I knew the pickets had not been taken off, as it was not light enough to see a man to distinguish friend from foe, any distance. The picket halted me before I got to the fence, and said: "Who comes there?" I said, "Friend, without the countersign." The next question was, "How did you come there?" and I answered, saying: "I was captured yesterday, and have been shot twice by guerrillas." "Where do you belong?" said the picket, and I answered: "Co. F, 130th Regiment Indiana Volunteers, Colonel C. S. Parrish, Third Brigade, Third Division, Twenty-third Army Corps." Said the picket: "We belong to that; advance, friend, with your hands up." And I did so, but I could not get over the fence, and they said: "Hold on until the relief comes up." They came and helped me over the fence. They asked if it was me the other relief had fired upon. I told them it was. They said the reason they had done so was because they had been attacked last night by guerrillas, and their orders were to fire on anything without halting it. I told them I had a partner out there some place. "I wish you would find him and tell him I am safe, and tell him to come on. Tell me how far it is to my regiment." "It is about one mile," said they; "you had better stop at General Cooper's headquarters and report." I did so. The first men I saw that I knew were Lieutenant W. H. Covert and Curtis Burgin from my company. They did not know me, and the first words they said were: "My God! pardner! what is the matter?" I told them in as short a way as I could, as it was very difficult and painful for me to talk. The General ordered one of them to put me on a horse and take me to my regiment. I told them I could walk better than I could ride, as the motion of the horse would give me much pain.

They were going to move the command, and were dividing it there; part of it going up Duck River under command of Gen. Cooper, and part under Col. Parrish was to remain there, consisting of two regiments—our own regiment and the 99th Ohio, and half of the artillery. I found my regiment on a large hill. When I arrived at the foot of the hill I could not go any further, so I laid down by the side of a path and said to myself, "That is the hardest mile I ever traveled." I had not lain there but a short time when one of my company boys, Ambrose Hammans, second duty seargeant, then acting as orderly sergeant, came down the hill after water, and he repeated the lieutenant's words, saying, "My God! pard, what is the matter? Where do you belong?" Said I, "I am Birt Crouse; I want you to help me up the hill; I can't talk much." He said, "I will go and call some of the boys; you are not fit to walk." He went to the top of the hill and fairly yelled: "Company F, Birt is down here and is all shot to pieces, and the worse sight you ever saw to be living, and he wants to get up the hill." I never will forget the way he sang this out, in his excited manner, and not only the company, but all that were within the sound of his voice came: some did not wait to dress, but as they had slept, some dressing as they ran, and better looking faces I thought I had never seen. They sympathized with me as much as brothers.

The regimental surgeon dressed my wounds and said to my captain, "Are you acquainted with his folks?" The captain said he was. Said the surgeon, "find out if he wants to send any word home, for he will never live to see 10 o'clock." The captain was a noble man, always ready to help any of his men out of trouble. He came and sat by me in the little dog tent and said, "Birt, I want to talk to you a little." I told my story as briefly as I could, and that I wanted him to send some men to find Grandstaff, "send a pretty good squad and arm them." I said, "and bring them to me before they go out, for I want to give them orders." He said, "Ambrose, detail thirty men and a sergeant, and see that their guns are all in good order." But he did not have to make the detail, he had more volunteers than he knew what to do with. They were furnished with forty rounds of ammunition to each man, and were brought to me for orders, and I said: "Boys, you are going in a particular place, you have never fought those villains, and so I say to you, boys, if you are attacked, fight for life, you can see how they have served me." And so they went.

"Birt," said the captain, "do you want to send any word home? If so, what is it? You can't live long." I said, "No, I am all right, if I can only get some rest. So please don't bother me." Our parents had lived near each other for many years, and when I enlisted he had promised my father that he would watch over me, and hence his anxiety to do something for me, and I had to send him away so often that at last I got so tired that I sent for the colonel, who was away when I was brought in, and knew nothing of my condition. And when he came to see me and learned what I wanted, he cried like a child, and asked what he could do for me. I told him I could not tell him how I felt, but, said I, "Colonel, I want rest; can you fix it so I can get it?" He said, "Yes," and turning to the captain, said: "We must put a guard over our boy, he begs so for rest, and I feel I must do all I can for him, for God knows he has seen enough." The guards were brought, and their orders were to allow no one but the man who waited upon me to come near me. So then I rested as well as could be expected, and I laid there until about 4 o'clock, but felt too bad to eat. They talked to me for a while, and I went to sleep and rested pretty well that night. In the morning, which was Tuesday, the 29th, my nurse, Robert G. Rogers, now living at Ossian, Ind., a noble fellow, got some corn meal and made a gruel, which he fed me with a spoon, and you may believe it tasted good, as I had eaten nothing since we were captured, which took place about 11 o'clock, Sunday, the 27th, as before stated.

We were at that time cut off from all communication, so we remained there for a few days and then started on a forced march for Franklin, Tenn. The squad of men who were sent out to hunt Grandstaff had been gone three days and had not found him, but on the fourth day we received a dispatch stating that he was up the river with the general's command, had the ball taken out, and was doing well. We had just so many hours in which to reach Franklin in order to get ahead of Hood, but did not make it, and so the battle of Franklin, or Columbia, as some called it, was fought.

We only got in sight of the town and captured one picket post; they did not fire a gun. We came to a halt and found the rebels lay around us in the shape of a horse shoe. It was about 10 o'clock at night when we captured the post and they were just starting their camp fires and supposed we were some of their own army moving. Our officers held a council how to get out; they were gathered around the wagon I was in, and I heard them say, "We can make a dash and get our men through, but we cannot get our artillery and wagons through;" and then they went away, and I went out of the back of that wagon, saying, "If this wagon is not going, I don't belong to it; where is my regiment?" "You have been there enough haven't you," says the Colonel, "but we are not going to go through. You stay in the wagon, and if we conclude to make the attempt I will come and let you know." But I was afraid they might forget me, so he directed me to my regiment. and directions were given us how to make a retrograde movement, and we did so. We got out of the horse shoe without any noise, no gun was fired, and not a mule brayed. We crossed the Cumberland River near Clarksville, Tenn., at which place I was put upon a hospital boat (we marched 84 miles after leaving the vicinity of Franklin), and I remained on the boat until I was able to do duty, which was about six months. and then I joined my regiment at Charlotte, N. C., in June, 1865. At the close of the war a partial account of our affair with the Bush-whackers was published in the Louisville Journal, the same being furnished by our boat surgeon.

Afterword

Editing the text of this little book was quite a bit more work than I had expected it to be, but it was also quite a bit more rewarding than I had anticipated.

My wife commented to me one day relatively early in our marriage that she had expected that she'd have to tell me to throw out some of those old books I had, but that she now saw that I actually reread them. Actually, I find it very interesting to revisit a book that I haven't read in many years, and to see how it compares with my recollection of it.

More often than not a book that I recalled with great fondness, or as having been simply brilliantly written or plotted leaves quite a different impression on me in the re-reading.

That has been true here, but not in the typical way:
I remembered this as a bit of an adventure story,
as a war story of the type that boys like to read,
as a ripping good yarn;
and so it is.
However, it is also quite a bit more than I had remembered.

As I write these words, we have just celebrated Memorial Day in the U.S. – Decoration Day as it was once called. That holiday's origin in the Civil War was all the more meaningful to me as I had just finished up the final proofreading of this text, with the story of the escape of Birt and Grandstaff from the guerrillas fresh in my mind.

To top it off, my church choir sang the Battle Hymn of the Republic at the Sunday Service with all its attendant Civil War associations.

Add in my son's current Army service (which I mentioned in the introduction), and it really should have come as no surprise to me that I would be a bit more emotionally involved in the song than in years past, but logic seldom comports with emotion – at least in my experience.

Although Birt's story of his capture by and escape from the Confederate guerrillas offers all the opportunity one could ever want to complain about the Generals and politicians forcing the common man to fight the wars, it seems never to even occur to him to do so. Rather we get the story of a man (of a boy, really) who wanted to serve his country, who truly believed in the cause for which he had volunteered, and who would no more have gone home before the job was done than to switch sides because he liked grey uniforms better than blue.

It's a story of true patriotism, humanity, and heroism. Birt makes no bones about his being afraid, of begging for his life, but at the same time, he goes on, doing his duty to his country and to his fellows. This little book gives us quite a nice look at what it really means to be a hero – to continue doing your duty, even when you're afraid to do it – and that's something that's sorely needed in this and in every time.

At any rate, I think that my great-great-grandfather's little book holds up nicely all these years later, and I hope you have enjoyed reading it as much as I have in bringing it back into print.

Charles J. van Becelaere
June 2010